LATINO CELEBRATIONS

CELEBRATING
DAY OF
THE DEAD!

MARISA ORGULLO

PowerKiDS press

New York

Published in 2019 by The Rosen Publishing Group, Inc.
29 East 21st Street, New York, NY 10010

First Edition

Editor: Brianna Battista
Book Design: Reann Nye

Photo Credits: Cover (child) Sollina Images/Blend Images/Getty Images; cover (background) Christian Kober/robertharding/Getty Images; p. 5 Dina Julayeva/Shutterstock.com; p. 7 Werner Forman/Universal Images Group/Getty Images; p. 9 Lokibaho/iStock Unreleased/Getty Images; p. 11 FREDERIC J. BROWN/AFP/Getty Images; p. 13 Carlos Ivan Palacios/Shutterstock.com; p. 15 Angela Ostafichuk/Shutterstock.com; p. 17 AGCuesta/Shutterstock.com; p. 19 Wu Swee Ong/Moment/Getty Images; p. 21 J Pat Carter/Getty Images News/Getty Images; p. 22 BestStockFoto/Shutterstock.com.

Library of Congress Cataloging-in-Publication Data

Names: Orgullo, Marisa, author.
Title: Celebrating Day of the Dead! / Marisa Orgullo.
Description: New York : PowerKids Press, [2019] | Series: Viva! Latino celebrations | Includes index.
Identifiers: LCCN 2018025626| ISBN 9781538342145 (Library bound) | ISBN 9781538342121 (Paperback) | ISBN 9781538342138 (6 pack)
Subjects: LCSH: All Souls' Day–Mexico–Juvenile literature. | All Souls' Day–Latin America–Juvenile literature. | Mexico–Social life and customs–Juvenile literature. | Latin America–Social life and customs–Juvenile literature.
Classification: LCC GT4995.A4 O74 2019 | DDC 394.266–dc23
LC record available at https://lccn.loc.gov/2018025626

Manufactured in the United States of America

CPSIA Compliance Information: Batch Batch #CWPK19: For Further Information contact Rosen Publishing, New York, New York at 1-800-237-9932

CONTENTS

Joy in Remembering

Every autumn, a beautiful holiday takes place in Mexico and Latin America. On the first two days of November, families gather to remember their loved ones who have died. However, the gathering isn't sad. It is filled with food, music, and love! This holiday is called Día de los Muertos, or Day of the Dead.

On Day of the Dead, people come together and remember their loved ones who have passed away.

Day of the Dead has been celebrated for hundreds of years! Early groups of people living in what is now Mexico, including the Aztecs, believed that the spirits of the dead traveled back to Earth once a year. These groups left offerings of flowers and fruit to help the spirits of their loved ones along in the **journey**.

Shown here is a statue of Mictecacihuatl, a goddess that the Aztecs called "Lady of the Dead."

Many groups celebrate loved ones who have died. Many **Catholics** remember their dead on November 1 and 2—All Saints' Day and All Souls' Day. When Spanish Catholics came to Mexico in the 1500s, the two celebrations became mixed together. Together, they became Day of the Dead.

When Catholics arrived from Spain, they built missions, or churches, in new countries to spread their beliefs.

Honoring the Dead

To honor loved ones on Day of the Dead, many families set up an *ofrenda* (oh-FREN-duh), an **altar** to remember loved ones. They place photos of the dead there. Children write notes and draw pictures. Sometimes *ofrendas* are set up at home. Sometimes they are at the loved one's **grave**. Families gather around the *ofrenda* and think about happy **memories**.

Candles are an important part of an *ofrenda*. One candle is lit for each loved one being remembered.

Ofrendas have more than just photos and notes. They are often full of gifts and toys such as skulls, or **skeleton** heads. Rows of colorful paper cutouts called *papel picado* (pa-PEL pee-KAH-thoh) fly from strings. Bright flowers called marigolds welcome the spirits. Sometimes the flowers are laid out between the graves and the *ofrendas,* helping to guide the spirits to their families.

On Day of the Dead, people spend time cleaning and decorating the graves of their loved ones.

Food for the Spirits

Food is an important part of Day of the Dead. On this holiday, families cook foods that their loved ones liked. They feast on **tamales** made with meat, cheese, or nuts. They snack on fruit and sweets. Some families pack up the feast and take it to eat by a loved one's grave.

These candies are called sugar skulls. They're very sweet!

Bakers have a big job on Day of the Dead! When the holiday arrives, bakers sell *pan de muerto* (PAHN DEH MWER-toh), or bread of the dead. Many bakers put a small, round piece on top of each bread. This piece is meant to look like a skull. On the sides, they put skinny pieces of bread that are meant to look like bones.

This is what *pan de muerto* looks like. The tops are dusted with sugar!

This celebration is a time to make people laugh. People write short stories that make fun of famous men and women. Artists dress skeletons in clothes and position them in ways that make them look like they're playing soccer, shopping, or driving! It's also a holiday full of music. People sing and play **instruments**.

This character, called La Catrina, is everywhere during Day of the Dead in Mexico.

The United States has many Latin American and Mexican families. Thanks to them, Day of the Dead is being celebrated here more often. Mexican Americans build *ofrendas* and eat *pan de muerto*. Children play with paper skeletons. Mexican Americans and other Latinos celebrate their family members who have died, even if they aren't close to their graves.

Dancers take part in a Día de los Muertos parade in Oklahoma City.

Some people think that Day of the Dead is like Halloween. The skeletons can seem scary, and talking about death might be hard. However, Latin Americans find great joy in this holiday. They remember the people they once knew and still love now. Day of the Dead is a special time to celebrate life and those we share it with.

GLOSSARY

altar: A table or a stone on which offerings are made.

Catholic: Belonging or relating to the church that is led by the pope.

grave: A place where a dead person is buried.

instrument: An object used to make music.

journey: An act of traveling from one place to another.

memory: Something remembered about the past.

skeleton: The bones that give animals' or people's bodies shape.

tamale: Cornmeal dough rolled with ground meat or beans and seasoning, wrapped in corn husks, and steamed.

INDEX

WEBSITES

Due to the changing nature of Internet links, PowerKids Press has developed
an online list of websites related to the subject of this book. This site is updated
regularly. Please use this link to access the list: www.powerkidslinks.com/lcila/dead